DESKTOP

Horseshoes

RP Minis®
Hachette Book Group
1290 Avenue of the Americas, New York, NY 10104
www.runningpress.com
@Running_Press

First Mini Kit Edition: September 2009

Published by RP Minis, an imprint of Perseus Books,
LLC, a subsidiary of Hachette Book Group, Inc. The RP
Minis name and logo is a registered trademark of the
Hachette Book Group.

ISBN: 978-0-7624-3635-4 (First Mini Kit Edition),
978-0-7624-9946-5 (Revised Edition)

Contents

05 Introduction

07 Horseshoes through the Years

13 Getting Started

27 Let's Play

37 Conclusion

INTRO-DUCTION

Unwind and experience the fun of horseshoes anytime, anywhere with this miniature desktop version of the classic game! With *Desktop Horseshoes*, you can beat the heat, conquer the cold, and stimulate the mind and body—it might even boost your productivity. Saddle up to your desk solo or grab a colleague or friend and let the games begin!

HORSESHOES
THROUGH THE
Years

Horseshoe pitching can be traced back to Roman soldiers in the 14th century, who tossed metal rings over stakes pounded in the ground for recreational use. The game also has its origins in quoits, which is a version of the old Grecian game of discus throwing. Quoits are disks with a hole in the middle that might have at one time been used as weapons. The game involves throwing the disks over a pin implanted in clay.

Another theory is that Grecian armies who couldn't afford the discus took discarded iron plates or rings that had been nailed on horses' shoes, set up a stake, and began throwing at it; when the game evolved to include two stakes isn't exactly known.

Horseshoe pitching seemed to have been a favorite among soldiers in many wars for centuries, and upon returning home from combat they shared the game with family and friends, thus broadening its popularity and utility. In fact, the National Horseshoe Pitchers Association (NHPA) as it is known today derived from mule shoe throwing in the Union Camps during the Civil War.

Pitching courts sprung up in hundreds of cities, villages, and farming communities and by the 1920s, horseshoe pitching was a popular family sport and both winter and summer world championship tournaments were held every year.

Today, horseshoe pitching continues to grow in popularity, particularly in the United States and Canada. Along with world championships in six classes including men, women, boys, girls, senior men, and elders, it is estimated that more than 15 million people enjoy the game—whether it's played in a tournament, league, public recreation area, or in the good ol' backyard.

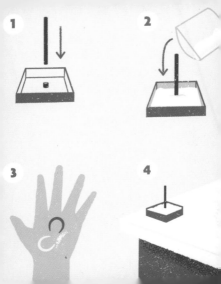

★ Getting STARTED ★

Now that we've outlined some of the fascinating history of horseshoes, you're ready to get a little competition of your own started! Let's set the stakes (in more ways than one), and get acquainted with the equipment and fundamentals of the game—scaled down to miniature!

EQUIPMENT

If you are at all familiar with a traditional game of horseshoes, the horseshoe pitch consists of two ends, each of which has a "pitching box." Inside each pitching box is a smaller rectangle referred to as the "pit," which is filled with sand to absorb the impact of a horseshoe. In the middle of the pit a "stake" sticks up above the surface, which is usually inclined slightly towards the thrower (please note the stake in this miniature version is not inclined like a standard size stake but should be vertical).

Desktop Horseshoes conveniently comes complete with all the equipment you need to set up game virtually anywhere and on a moment's notice:

* 1 "pitching box"
* 1 metal "stake" that screws into the bottom of pitching box
* 4 metal horseshoes
* a bag of sand

First, firmly screw the stake into the hole in the middle of the pitching box until secure. Next, fill the box with sand evenly until it comes to just below the edge of the box. Grab your horseshoes (two for you and two for a friend or co-worker, or all four for yourself if "flying" solo), find a desktop or an appropriate flat surface free from obstruction, and you're ready to throw!

FUNDAMENTALS

Ok, wait, hold your horses (I mean, horseshoes!). Before you start throwing, we advise that you consider a few fundamentals to improve your pitching skills. Even though a horseshoe may symbolize luck, there is little or no luck involved in pitching ringers!

NOTE: these pointers generally apply to the full-size game of horseshoes, but they have been slightly adapted to apply to our miniature, desktop version as well!

GRIP

Your grip should be firm, but should also remain flexible. Holding onto the shoe too tightly before release may result in it turning too much or flipping in the air. However, if you aren't holding onto the shoe tight enough, it might not turn enough or it might slip from your fingers before it's even released!

BODY POSITION

Stand (or sit, if at your desk) with your body erect, keeping your muscles free from tension. In traditional horseshoes, pitchers take on a slight crouch so if standing, you might want to assume that position. The pitcher should stand or sit to one side of the pit, on a line about even with the stake. A right-handed player should position themselves to the left of the stake, a left-hander should be on the right-hand side of it. The goal is to keep your arm in line with the stake to achieve the best result (i.e. a ringer).

SWING

Even though it is called horseshoe "pitching," the horseshoes aren't really "pitched," they are swung. The "swing" is comprised of three parts: the back-swing, front-swing, and follow-through. The most difficult of all the fundamentals to master, the swing is what determines the distance of the horseshoe. A lot of horseshoe pitchers lack ability with this skill as all too often they don't take the time to develop their swings fully. Practice makes perfect, so find one that works for you!

FOLLOW-THROUGH

The follow-through is the continuation of the swing that completes a circle, which is achieved by the hand continuing to move toward the stake after it releases the horseshoe. The follow-through is the short distance traveled by the hand between the release and where it begins to rise above the head.

TIMING AND RHYTHM

Rhythm, the dominant fundamental in sports, and timing are both needed to regulate the movement of all the combined fundamentals to execute a successful delivery of the horseshoe to the stake.

Don't try to master all the fundamentals at once; each one must be worked on and practiced individually. While the object of the game is to make ringers, don't focus all your attention on that one goal—with the knowledge of the game and practice, you will have the confidence and ability to be a winner!

Let's PLAY

The rules of horseshoe pitching vary greatly, depending on the country, area, or town in which it is played... and now have been slightly adapted for desktop play!

RULES OF THE GAME

NOTE: these are instructions for friendly play and are not a complete set of standard regulations. If you're not sure what the set of rules are, we advise that you play by house (or in this case, desk) rules!

The game starts with a coin toss to determine who goes first. Each player then stands (or sits) to one side to the opposite pit they are throwing to; which side is determined by what hand they throw with. The player throws both horseshoes, one after the other. The second player then throws their two shoes.

The game is divided into innings. Each inning is comprised of four horseshoe pitches, two by each player. The score for the inning is calculated by the players walking to the opposite pit to determine the score and retrieve their shoes. If playing *Desktop Horseshoes*, it is likely that it is just a matter or stretching your arms out to calculate your score and retrieve your shoes! The players play the next inning by reversing direction and throwing at the other stake in the same fashion.

SCORING

An official game of traditional horseshoes is played to 40 points, but for *Desktop Horseshoes*, we recommend playing to 21. Just make sure the number is set before the first shoe is thrown. The first player to reach or surpass the pre-determined number is the winner!

A ringer (the main objective) is a horseshoe that completely surrounds the stake, and it is worth three points. Just because you score a ringer, though, doesn't always mean you get to keep the points—it depends on how your opponent performs! If the other player scores a ringer on

their turn in the same inning, it can-cels out your ringer so no points are scored. Alternatively, if there are no ringers, or only one ringer thrown out of the four throws, the next clos-est horseshoe to the stake counts as one point.

Scoring can get complicated due to the way in which ringers are cancelled out, so here are some scenarios to illustrate how points are scored in a traditional (or desktop) game of horseshoes:

- If both players throw one ringer, the ringers are cancelled out and the closer of the other two horseshoes to the stake scores one point.
- If neither player throws a ringer, the closest horseshoe to the stake is scored as one point.
- If the first player scores a ringer but the second player scores two ringers, the second player earns three points.

- If only one ringer has been scored by the two players, that player wins three points and adds one more point to their score if their second horseshoe is the closest of the remaining three.
- If a player throws two ringers and the opponent scores none, the first player earns six points.

The first player to reach 21 points wins the game; the loser has to go on a coffee run.

★ *Conclusion* ★

Many sports fans think of horseshoes as nothing more than a backyard barbeque sport. Now, with *Desktop Horseshoes* you can bring the outdoor game indoors to a desk near you and the fun is literally right at your fingertips. Rest assured you'll be a ringer in no time... you can stake your lucky horseshoe on it!

This book has been bound using
handcraft methods and Smyth-sewn
to ensure durability.
Written by Lindsay Rosoff.
Designed by Celeste Joyce.
Illustrated by James Olstein.